ESSEN
WOR

# DRAWING
# WITH WORD

# ABOUT THIS BOOK

*Drawing with Word* is an easy-to-follow guide to some of the more sophisticated features of Microsoft's® Word 2000 word-processing program to create highly illustrated documents.

WORD 2000 IS BEST KNOWN AS THE leading word-processing program available for the PC. Most people are aware that Word also contains a drawing capability, which for various reasons is not as well understood as it deserves to be. This book attempts to redress that deficiency. To get the best from this book, some knowledge of the program will be useful. You will still be able to work through the operations shown, even if you are new to Word, but you might find it useful first to read the accompanying volume, *Designing Documents*, which deals with the program's more basic features.

*Drawing with Word* takes a step-by-step approach to mastering some of the more advanced features of the program. Almost every step is accompanied by an illustration showing you how your own screen should look at each point. The first

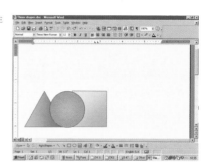

chapter explains the various toolbars, and it is worth studying these in order to use Word efficiently.

The book contains several features to help you understand both what is happening and what you need to do.

Command keys, such as ENTER and CTRL, are shown in these rectangles: [Enter ⏎] and [Ctrl], so that there's no confusion, for example, over whether you should press that key or type the letters "ctrl."

Cross-references are shown in the text as left- or right-hand page icons: and . The page number and the reference are shown at the foot of the page.

In addition to the step-by-step sections, there are boxes that explain features in detail, and tip boxes that provide you with alternative methods. Finally, at the back you will find a glossary of common terms and a comprehensive index.

ESSENTIAL **DK** COMPUTERS

WORD PROCESSING

# DRAWING WITH WORD

JOHN WATSON

## LONDON, NEW YORK, MUNICH, MELBOURNE, DELHI

SENIOR EDITOR Jacky Jackson
SENIOR ART EDITOR Sarah Cowley
DTP DESIGNER Julian Dams and Rajen Shah
PRODUCTION CONTROLLER Melanie Dowland

MANAGING EDITOR Adèle Hayward
MANAGING ART EDITOR Karen Self
CATEGORY PUBLISHER Stephanie Jackson

Produced for Dorling Kindersley Limited by
Design Revolution Limited, Queens Park Villa,
30 West Drive, Brighton, East Sussex BN2 0QW
EDITORIAL DIRECTOR Ian Whitelaw
SENIOR DESIGNER Andrew Easton
PROJECT EDITOR Julie Whitaker
DESIGNER Paul Bowler

First published in Great Britain in 2000 by
Dorling Kindersley Limited,
80 Strand, London WC2R 0RL

Revised edition 2002
A Penguin publication

2  4  6  8  10  9  7  7  5  3  1

A CIP catalogue record for this book is available from the British Library.

ISBN 0-7513-4634-9

Colour reproduced by Colourscan, Singapore
Printed and bound in Italy by Graphicom

For our complete catalogue visit
www.dk.com

# Contents

# THE DRAWING TOOLS

The tools that are used in drawing with Word are all contained
in dedicated toolbars, although some of the formatting
commands are carried out by using the Formatting toolbar.

## WHAT CAN I DRAW WITH WORD?

Word-processing programs once did
exactly that – simply processed words.
However, the features that have evolved
and are now contained in Microsoft Word
2000 go far beyond the original, and
limited, capabilities of early text
processing. Microsoft Word does not
pretend to be a leading-edge, graphics-
development tool. Instead, it contains the
essential means for enhancing your
documents with tools to create basic lines,
curves, and freehand shapes. In addition,
Word contains predesigned shapes that
can be resized and layered to suit
particular needs. Once the basic shapes
have been created, there are several effects
that can be applied to them including
highly flexible 3-D effects, lighting,
shadows, colors, and the integration of
text and graphics.

### FLEXIBLE INTEGRATION

With the integration of
formattable text and
extremely flexible graphics
manipulation, Microsoft
Word gives you the
opportunity to combine
images and words in ways
that will suit the demands
of most small-scale docu-
ment production.

# THE EFFECTS TOOLBARS

Two of the effects that are available when drawing with Word are the 3-D effect and the shadow effect. Both of these effects have their own toolbars containing buttons for modifying the effect. The toolbars are accessed via their respective buttons on the **Drawing** toolbar, then clicking on **Settings** in the pop-up menu.

## 3-D SETTINGS TOOLBAR

This toolbar lets you control aspects of the 3-D effect, such as tilt, the depth and direction of the 3-D effect, how the object is illuminated, and its surface texture and color.

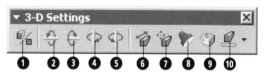

### THE 3-D SETTINGS TOOLBAR

| | |
|---|---|
| ❶ 3-D On/Off | ❻ Depth |
| ❷ Tilt Down | ❼ Direction |
| ❸ Tilt Up | ❽ Lighting |
| ❹ Tilt Left | ❾ Surface |
| ❺ Tilt Right | ❿ 3-D Color |

## SHADOW SETTINGS TOOLBAR

Applying a shadow to a drawing object is an alternative method of adding depth to the object. The toolbar provides tools to move and color the shadow effect.

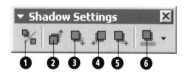

### THE SHADOW SETTINGS TOOLBAR

| | |
|---|---|
| ❶ Shadow On/Off | ❹ Nudge Shadow Left |
| ❷ Nudge Shadow Up | ❺ Nudge Shadow Right |
| ❸ Nudge Shadow Down | ❻ Shadow Color |

9 **The drawing toolbar**

# THE WORD TOOLBARS

The two principal toolbars that are used in drawing with Word are the **Formatting** toolbar and the **Drawing** toolbar. In the context of using Word to create drawings, the **Formatting** toolbar is mainly used to format text when it is being integrated with graphics or images. The **Drawing** toolbar contains all the tools that you are likely to need to create shapes, incorporate images, change line styles, and select a variety of effects to add to your drawings. There is no need to attempt to memorize each of these commands; the important factor is to be aware that they are available.

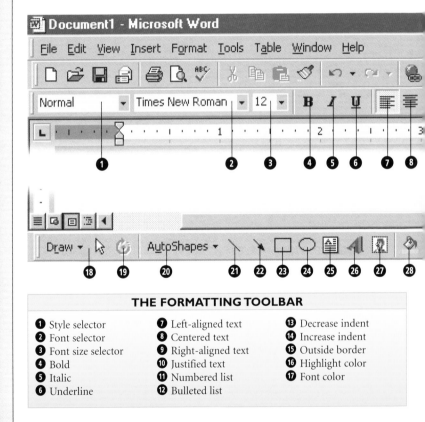

## THE FORMATTING TOOLBAR

| | | |
|---|---|---|
| **1** Style selector | **7** Left-aligned text | **13** Decrease indent |
| **2** Font selector | **8** Centered text | **14** Increase indent |
| **3** Font size selector | **9** Right-aligned text | **15** Outside border |
| **4** Bold | **10** Justified text | **16** Highlight color |
| **5** Italic | **11** Numbered list | **17** Font color |
| **6** Underline | **12** Bulleted list | |

## TOOLBAR LAYOUT

For a variety of reasons that depend on settings, the toolbars and ruler in Word may adopt any one of a number of different layouts. If Word doesn't show the **Formatting** toolbar above the ruler as shown here, first place the cursor over the **Formatting** toolbar "handle" at the end of the toolbar. When the four-headed arrow appears, (right) hold down the mouse button, and drag the toolbar into position.

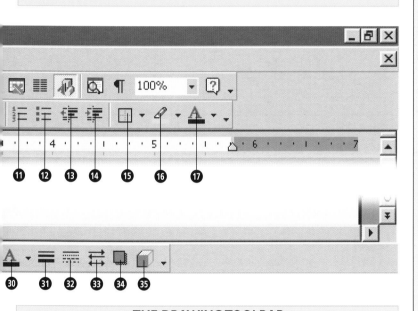

## THE DRAWING TOOLBAR

18 Select objects
19 Free rotate
20 AutoShapes menu
21 Line
22 Arrow
23 Rectangle

24 Oval
25 Text box
26 Insert WordArt
27 Insert Clip Art
28 Fill color
29 Line color

30 Font color
31 Line style
32 Dash style
33 Arrow style
34 Shadow effects
35 3-D effects

# LINES AND CURVES

The name that Word 2000 gives to all the marks and shapes used in drawing with Word is "drawing objects." The most common drawing objects that you will use are lines and curves.

## PRINT LAYOUT VIEW AND THE DRAWING TOOLBAR

When working only with text in Word, it is usually enough to use the **Normal** view. But when drawing in Word 2000, your document needs to be displayed in **Print Layout View**. Select this option either from the **View** drop-down menu or from the **Print Layout View** button at the bottom-left of the document window.

### THE DRAWING TOOLBAR

● The majority of the actions to be carried out in drawing with Word are selected from the Drawing toolbar. You can display this toolbar in one of several ways. The first is to click on **View** in the Menu bar, select **Toolbars**, and click on **Drawing** in the submenu.

● The **Drawing** toolbar
can also be displayed by
clicking on the **Drawing**
button on the **Standard**
toolbar.

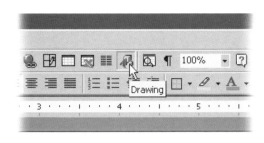

● Alternatively, right-click
on an empty area of a
toolbar and click on the
**Drawing** option from the
menu that appears.

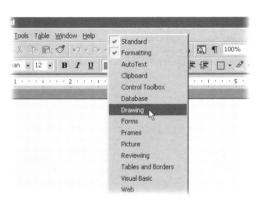

● When the toolbar
appears, it may be
"floating" in the document
window. You might find it
easier to work if the toolbar
is "docked" at the foot of
the window. To do this,
place the cursor over the
blue title bar at the top of
the toolbar. Hold down the
left mouse button and drag
the toolbar until it locks
into position below the
document window.

# DRAWING THE LINES

The **AutoShapes** button on the **Drawing** toolbar contains most of the drawing objects that you will use. The objects range from simple lines to shapes that are tailor-made for specific uses, but lines and freeforms are where most people begin.

## 1 SELECTING THE LINE OPTION

● To draw a line, begin by clicking on **AutoShapes** in the **Drawing** toolbar.

● In the pop-up menu, select **Lines** and click the **Line** button in the submenu.

● The menu closes and the arrow cursor changes to a cross hair cursor.

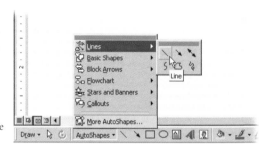

● Move the cross hair to the position where you want the line to begin, hold down the left mouse button, drag the cursor to the point where the line is to end, and release the mouse button.

● The line appears on the page with handles at either end and an anchor icon on the left-hand edge of the page. The handles can be clicked on to resize and move the line. The anchor indicates whether the line is locked to another object or to a paragraph.

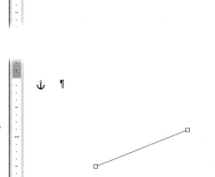

## 2 INSERTING A CURVE

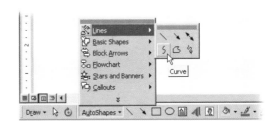

● To draw a curve, click on **AutoShapes** on the **Drawing** toolbar, select **Lines**, and then click on the **Curve** button.

● Click where you want the curve to begin, drag the mouse to start the curve, and left-click where you want the curve to bend.

● To finish drawing the curve, double-click with the mouse. (If you want to close the shape, click near its starting point.) The curve then appears surrounded by eight handles.

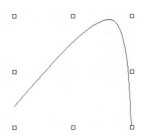

● Click off the curve to deselect it.

# FREEFORM DRAWING OBJECTS

Lines and curves have their uses, but they also have their limitations as far as flexibility is concerned. Word contains a feature, called freeform, which allows you to combine both straight lines and curves in one drawing object. However, it is notoriously difficult to achieve perfect results with a freeform at the first attempt.

### SELECTING FREEFORM

● On the **Drawing** toolbar, select **AutoShapes**, select **Lines**, and then select **Freeform**.

● Move the cursor to the position on the page where the freeform is to begin.

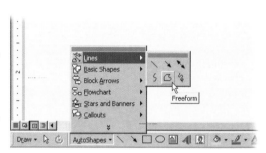

● To draw a straight line section of the freeform, left-click once, and drag the mouse.

● To draw a curved section freehand, hold down the left mouse button, the cursor changes to a pencil, and drag to draw a shape.

● The freeform can be ended either as an open shape, where the ends do not meet, or as a closed shape, where they do.

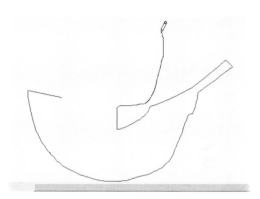

### *Finishing an open freeform*

To finish drawing an open freeform, double-click the left mouse button. The freeform disappears briefly while Word computes its shape and then it reappears.

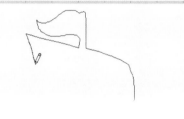

● The method of finishing a closed shape once the endpoint reaches the starting point depends on whether you are in freehand mode or are drawing a straight line.

● If you are in freehand mode with the mouse button held down, release the mouse button. If you are drawing a straight line when closing the shape, left-click once.

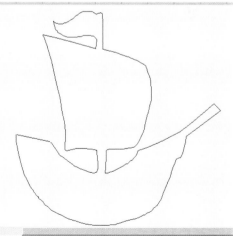

# RESHAPING FREEFORMS

The first results that are produced by using Word's freeform tool always need further work to improve them. This is done by either adding or deleting edit points, and by dragging either the edit points or their handles.

## 1 USING EDIT POINTS

● Select the freeform by placing the cursor over a section of the line that makes up the freeform, and the cursor changes to a four-way arrow. Click once with the left mouse button, and the resizing handles appear.

● On the **Drawing** toolbar, click on **Draw** and select **Edit Points**.

● A number of small black rectangles appears on the freeform at points known as vertexes, which mark either the extremity of a curve or the start and end points of a straight line.

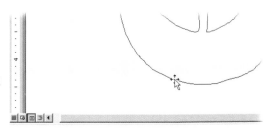

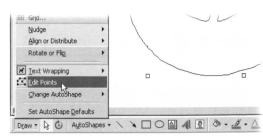

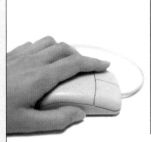

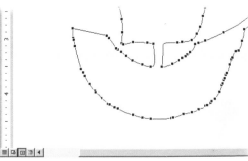

## 2 WORKING PRECISELY

● To increase the accuracy of your work, increase the screen magnification in the **Zoom Control** box to 500 percent. You can also slow the tracking speed of your mouse in the **Control Panel**, which is available through the **Start** button. This will give you greater control over the final shape.

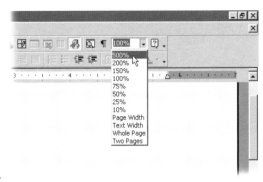

● Place the cursor over the vertex you want to modify. The cursor changes to a small open rectangle with four small directional arrows around it.

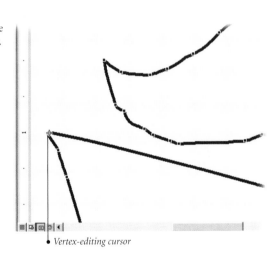

*Vertex-editing cursor*

● Hold down the left mouse button and drag the vertex to a new position. A red, dashed line appears showing the changes to the shape that you are making.

● Release the mouse button when the vertex has been repositioned. The curve takes on its new shape, and two blue lines appear on either side of the vertex ending in a handle.

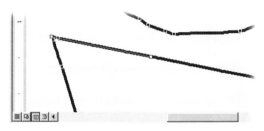

● Click on one of the handles at the end of one of the blue lines and hold down the mouse button. Now, by dragging the mouse, you can alter the degree of the curve in relation to the next vertex along the line.

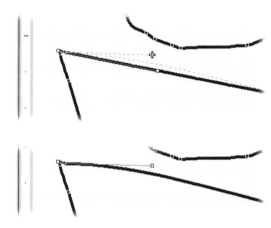

## 3 ADD AND DELETE A VERTEX

● You may want to change the shape of a line at a position where no vertex exists.

● To add a vertex, place the cursor where you want to position one, hold down the mouse button, and drag the line to its new location. New vertexes do not have handles with which you can alter the degree of curve.

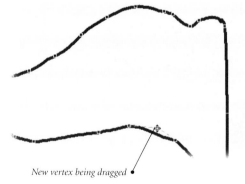

*New vertex being dragged* ●

● To delete a vertex, place the cursor over the vertex and hold down the [Ctrl] key. The cursor changes to an X-shape.

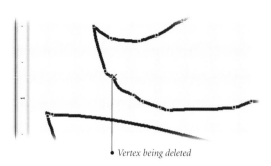

*Vertex being deleted*

● Click once to delete the vertex, and the line follows a new curve between the two vertexes that were on either side of the deleted vertex.

● Below is the finished drawing.

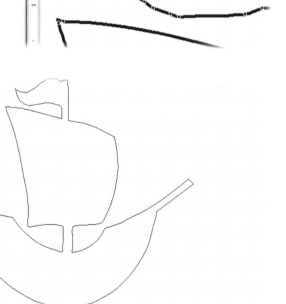

# USING ENCLOSED SHAPES

The most commonly used shapes in drawing in Word are enclosed shapes. As well as standard circles, ovals, squares, and rectangles, there are a number of other shapes available.

## OVALS AND RECTANGLES

The most basic enclosed shapes are ovals and rectangles. Word contains buttons on the **Drawing** toolbar that allow these shapes to be drawn and then resized, by using their handles, according to the requirements of your document and text.

### 1 ADDING OVALS

● To add an oval shape, click on the **Oval** button on the **Drawing** toolbar.
● As you move the cursor onto the document, the cursor changes into a cross hair. Place the cursor at the approximate point where you want the oval to appear. Hold down the left mouse button and drag the mouse to draw the oval.
● Release the mouse button when the oval is the size you want. The oval appears surrounded by eight handles.
● Click off the oval to remove the handles from the display.

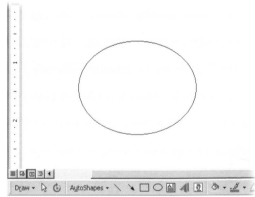

## 2 ADDING RECTANGLES

● To add a rectangle, click on the **Rectangle** button on the **Drawing** toolbar.

● Place the cursor where you want one of the corners of the rectangle to appear on the page. Hold down the left mouse button and drag the mouse to draw the rectangle.

● Release the mouse button when the rectangle is the size you want.

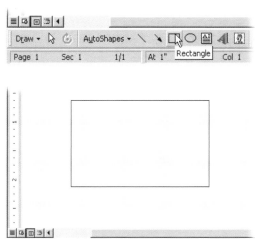

# INSERTING AN AUTOSHAPE

There are a number of predesigned shapes, known as **AutoShapes**, that are available in Word. From this wide range of shapes, you can select and draw the shape, then resize and reshape it according to what you need.

### AUTOSHAPE SELECTION

● Click **AutoShapes** on the **Drawing** toolbar, point to **Basic Shapes**, and from the menu that appears, select a shape by clicking on it.

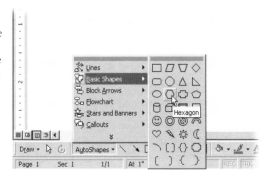

● Position the cursor in the document window where the shape is to appear, hold down the left mouse button and drag the mouse to draw the shape.

● Release the mouse button when you have the required shape.

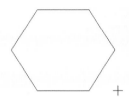

*Predefined sizes*
To insert an enclosed shape with a predefined size, select the shape and simply left-click in the document window.

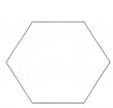

# RESIZING AUTOSHAPES

Autoshapes can be resized by using one of several methods. Precise resizing can be done via a dialog box, where you can also preserve the height and width ratio of the shape. Other resizing options include vertical, horizontal, and from the center.

## 1 RESIZING BY A PERCENTAGE

● Select the autoshape that you want to resize by placing the cursor either over one of its lines or within the shape and left-clicking.

● From the **Format** menu, click on **AutoShape** in the drop-down menu.

● The **Format AutoShape** dialog box opens with several tabs along the top, which contain different options. Click on the **Size** tab to the right of the **Colors and Lines** tab.

*The Size tab* ●

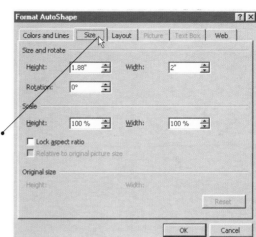

● Under **Scale**, enter the percentages that you want in the **Height** and **Width** boxes and click on **OK**.

● To retain the ratio in the autoshape between its height and width when using this resizing method, place a check mark in the **Lock aspect ratio** check box on the **Size** tab.

● The autoshape has been resized.

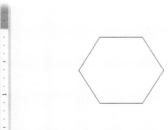

## 2 KEEPING OTHER PROPORTIONS

There are several combinations of keys that allow you to retain the proportion of your auto-shapes when resizing them.

● To maintain the ratio between the autoshape's width and height, hold down the ⟨⇧ Shift⟩ key while you drag a corner handle. In each of these resizing methods, a dashed outline of the shape appears to show the extent of the resizing as you drag the mouse.

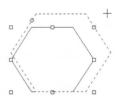

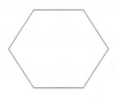

● To resize an autoshape vertically, horizontally, or diagonally from the center outward, hold down the ⟨Ctrl⟩ key and drag one of the handles.

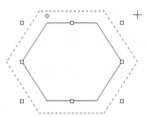

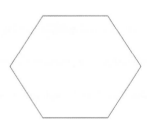

● Dragging one of the corner handles has the effect of stretching the autoshape.

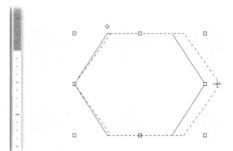

● However, if you wish to resize an autoshape proportionally from the center outward, hold down the [Ctrl] and [⇧ Shift] keys and drag a corner sizing handle.

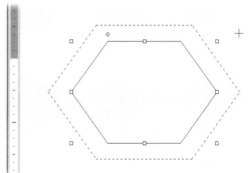

● The grab is resized without moving from its original center point.

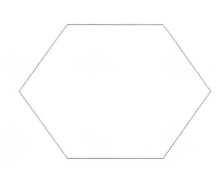

# DRAWING EFFECTS

Once you have inserted a drawing object into a document, there are a number of different effects that can be applied to it. The effects include colors, gradients, shadows, line colors, and 3-D.

## USING COLORS

Colors are known as "fills" in Microsoft Word as they fill an enclosed shape with the color that you select. There is a wide variety of colors from which to choose, and changing a color after using one is a very simple operation.

### 1 ADDING A COLOR

● Select the drawing object to which you want to add a color and click on the arrow next to the **Fill Color** button.

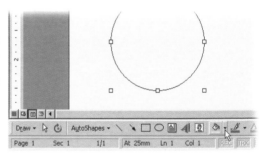

● A color palette pops up. Click on the color of your choice.

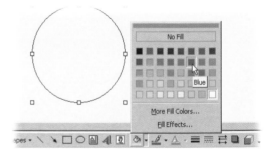

● The drawing object is filled with your selected color.

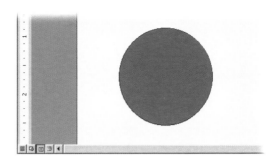

## 2 CHANGE A FILL COLOR

● Follow the previous steps and simply select another color from the palette. If you do not see the color you want, click on **More Fill Colors**.

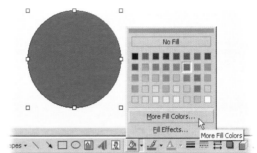

● The **Colors** dialog box opens. The **Standard** tab contains a hexagon of colors from which you can make your choice.

*The Standard tab* ●

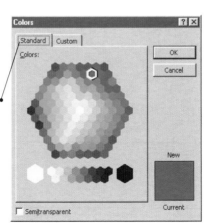

● The **Custom** tab contains a color pad. Drag the cursor across it and see the color change as you drag. Compare the new color with the current fill color in the color boxes at the bottom right.

*The **Custom** tab* ●

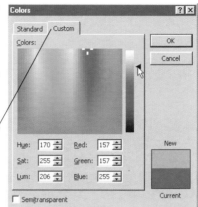

● Click on **OK** when you are satisfied with your selection.

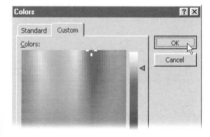

### *Remove a fill from a drawing object*

Select the drawing object that you want to change by clicking inside it. On the **Drawing** toolbar, click the arrow next to **Fill Color** and then click on **No Fill**. If you need to reselect an object once a fill has been removed, you'll need to click on the border of the object instead of inside it.

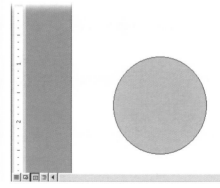

# COLORS AS GRADIENTS

Gradients, or "shades," allow a more subtle use of color. Normally a gradient shades from a lighter to darker tone, or from a darker to lighter tone. However, in Word, it is possible to shade from one color to a completely different color.

## 1 ADD A FILL EFFECT

● Select the drawing object that you want to change. On the **Drawing** toolbar, click the arrow next to **Fill Color** and click on **Fill Effects**.

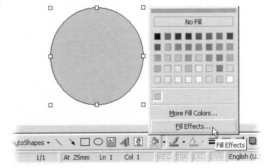

● The **Fill Effects** dialog box opens with four tabs along the top labeled **Gradient**, **Texture**, **Pattern**, and **Picture**.

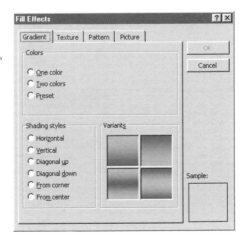

● In this example we'll use the options available under **Gradient**, also known as shade. The options on the other tabs work in a broadly similar way. In the **Shading styles** section of the **Gradient** tab, click on the **From center** radio button and click on **OK**.

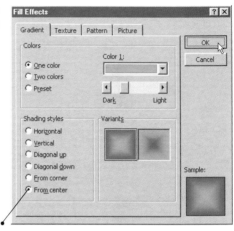

*From center button*

● The drawing object is now shaded with the lightest shade at the center and the heaviest at the perimeter.

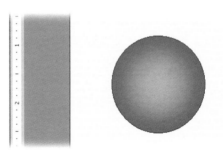

## 2 ADDING A SECOND COLOR

● With the drawing object still selected, display the **Gradient** tab again (as above) and click the **Two colors** radio button. A second color box, **Color 2**, appears.

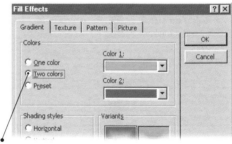

*Two colors button*

● Click on the down arrow to the right of the **Color 1** box and select a color.

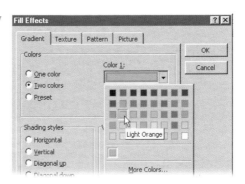

● Now click on the down arrow to the right of the **Color 2** box and select a second color.

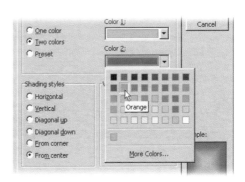

● In this example, with the gradient becoming darker toward the edges, a stronger effect is achieved if a light color is selected as the first (center) color, and a darker, but related, color is selected as the second color.

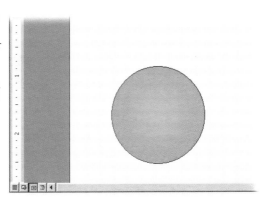

# SHADOWS FOR DRAWING OBJECTS

It is possible to add depth to the objects that you create using Word by placing a shadow either in front or behind them.

The color of the shadow, the direction in which the shadow falls, and the degree of shading can all be selected and controlled.

## 1 ADDING A SHADOW

● Begin by selecting the drawing object and, on the **Drawing** toolbar, click **Shadow**.

### *Shadow colors*
To see a wider range of colors, click on **More Shadow Colors** below the **Shadow Color** palette. The **Colors** dialog box opens, containing a wider range of colors.

● A pop-up menu appears, showing several shadow options.

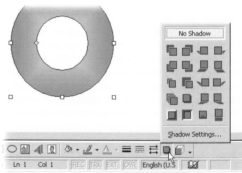

● As you place the cursor over an option, the number of the shadow style appears. Click on a shadow option to select and insert it into the document.

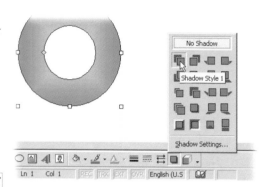

## SEMITRANSPARENT SHADOWS

It is possible to change the shadow color so you can see through it. Click on **Shadow Color** on the **Shadow Settings** toolbar and then click on **Semitransparent Shadow**. This is particularly useful if you have text behind the shadow because it then becomes readable rather than hidden.

## 2 CHANGING THE SHADOW COLOR

● Select the drawing object, click **Shadow** on the **Drawing** toolbar, and click on **Shadow Settings**.

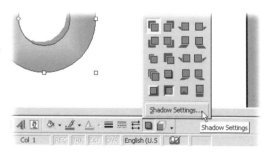

● The **Shadow Settings** toolbar appears. Click on the arrow next to **Shadow Color** and a pop-up palette appears. Click on the color you want.

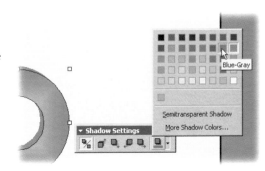

● The shadow is now colored with your selection.

## 3 CHANGING THE SHADOW OFFSET

● It is possible to change the position of the shadow in relation to the drawing object. This is known as the shadow offset. Follow the previous steps to display the **Shadow Settings** toolbar. The four center **Nudge Shadow** buttons on the toolbar can be used to nudge the shadow vertically or horizontally.

● Clicking the nudge buttons moves the shadow by 1 point (½ of an inch). To move the shadow by 6 points (½ of an inch), hold down the [⇧ Shift] key while clicking the nudge buttons. Here a combination of nudging the shadow up and to the left has been used to create a larger visible area of shadow.

# LINE COLORS AND LINE STYLES

By default, the borders of drawing objects in Word are marked by a black line. The principal controls that are available include changing the color of the line, changing the thickness of the line and, when required, removing the line.

## 1 ADDING A LINE COLOR

● To change the standard black line color of a drawing object, click on the object to select it. (The earlier shadow has been removed by clicking on the **No Shadow** option in the **Shadow** pop-up.) Click on the arrow next to **Line Color** and select one of the colors from the color palette that appears.

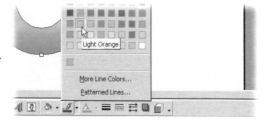

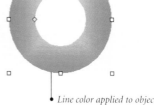

*Line color applied to object's edges*

● You can also click on
**More Line Colors** to open
the **Colors** dialog box if
you need a wider range of
colors.

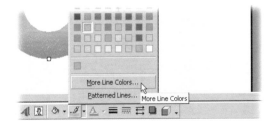

## 2 CHANGING THE LINE STYLE

● You can give a line a
different style, such as a
greater thickness, by
selecting the object, clicking
on **Line Style** on the
**Drawing** toolbar, and
selecting a style from the
pop-up menu.

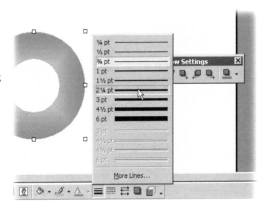

*Remove a line*
To remove a line from
around a drawing
object, display the **Line
Color** pop-up menu
and click on **No Line** at
the top of the menu.

# USING 3-D EFFECTS

A far more dramatic method of adding depth to your drawing objects is to apply a 3-D effect to them. Word provides a range of 3-D effects that can enhance virtually any shape you use or create, and they can be customized easily.

## 1 ADDING A 3-D EFFECT

● A 3-D effect is added to a drawing object by selecting the object, clicking on the **3-D** button on the **Drawing** toolbar, and then selecting one of the options from the pop-up menu.

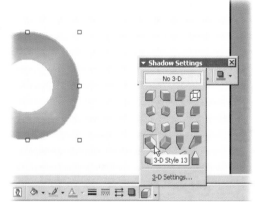

● Again, click off the object to see the effect. The 3-D effect is added to the object, which is also tilted in the direction of the chosen 3-D style.

## 2 CHANGING A 3-D EFFECT

● Select the drawing object and click the **3-D** button on the **Drawing** toolbar, then click **3-D Settings**.

● The **3-D Settings** toolbar appears; it contains several buttons with which you can alter the tilt, depth, lighting, surface appearance, and 3-D color.

● In this example, first we'll change the tilt of the object by clicking on the **Tilt Up** button repeatedly until the required tilt angle is reached.

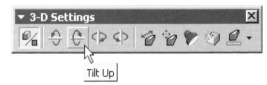

● It's the object itself that is tilted upward, not the 3D effect. This is why the object as a whole appears to tilt down while the "face" of the object tilts upward.

## 3 CHANGING THE LIGHTING EFFECT

● The appearance of a 3-D object can be changed dramatically by altering the way it is lit.

● Select the drawing object, click the **3-D** button on the **Drawing** toolbar, and click on **3-D Settings** on the pop-up menu to display the **3-D Settings** toolbar. Click on the **Lighting** button.

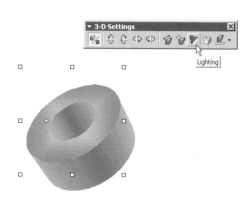

● On the drop-down menu, click on one of the buttons to select the direction from which the object is to be lit. Here, the option to light the object from below and from the left has been chosen.

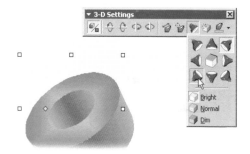

● The drop-down menu closes immediately after a selection has been made, and the drawing object now has a different light and shade effect.

● It is also interesting to experiment with the different lighting levels of **Bright**, **Normal**, and **Dim** that are available in the lighting drop-down menu.

# CONTROLLING OBJECTS

Once having created drawing objects and added effects to them,
there are several ways in which they can be controlled to
produce the design and layout that you need.

## LAYERING DRAWING OBJECTS

It's very likely that you will have more
than one drawing object in your
document, and it is likely that you will
want to position them in a preferred
order. Determining the order of objects
on the page is known as layering.

### 1 BRING AN OBJECT TO THE FRONT

● Select the object that you
want to move to the top
layer (in this case, the
circle) and, on the **Drawing**
toolbar, click on **Draw**,
choose **Order**, and then
**Bring to Front**.

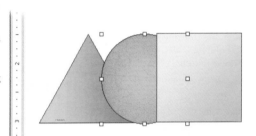

### HIDDEN OBJECTS

If the object is hidden
behind other objects,
select one object, then
press ⟨ Shift ⟩ + ⟨ Tab⇆ ⟩ to
select the drawing
objects in the order they
were created. The
hidden object is
eventually selected.

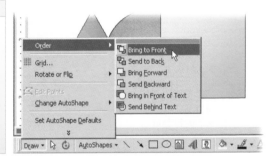

● In this case, the circle
now overlays the two other
objects. Click off the object
to see the effect.

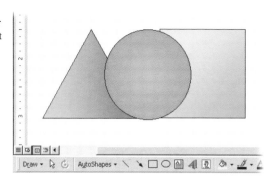

## 2 SEND AN OBJECT TO THE BACK

● Select the drawing object
that you want to move to
the lowest layer on the
document page, click on
**Draw** on the **Drawing**
toolbar, choose **Order**, and
click on **Send to Back**.

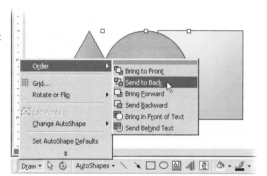

### OTHER LAYERS

In the **Order** commands
in the **Draw** button,
there are also
commands to change
the object's position by
only one layer – forward
or backward – and for
positioning an object
either behind or in front
of text.

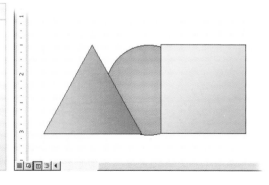

# ALIGNING AND ARRANGING

In addition to arranging drawing objects in relation to one another, it is also possible to align drawing objects along any of their edges, and align them in relation to the document page. Word contains many options to arrange objects by a combination of these criteria.

## 1 ALIGN OBJECTS BY THEIR EDGES

● When you are handling more than one drawing object at a time, you can select several drawing objects by holding down the ⇧Shift key as you select each one by clicking on it. Select each of the drawing objects to be aligned by their edges.

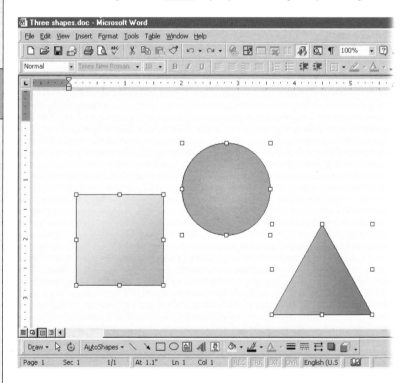

● Click on **Draw** on the **Drawing** toolbar and select **Align or Distribute**.

● In the submenu, the three center commands: **Align Top**, **Align Middle**, and **Align Bottom** move the selected objects vertically from their current positions to occupy the selected alignment. In this example, **Align Top** has been selected.

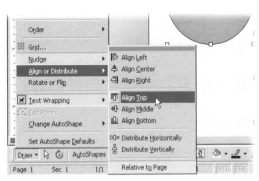

● Once **Align Top** has been selected, the objects move from their previous locations to new locations where the top parts of the objects are aligned.

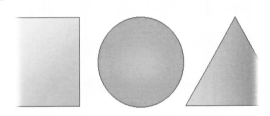

## 2 ALIGN OBJECTS ON THE PAGE

● It is also possible to align objects relative to the edges of the page. Select the objects you want to align, click **Draw** on the **Drawing** toolbar and select the **Align or Distribute** option. In the submenu, click on **Relative to Page** to ensure that the next alignment command aligns the objects in relation to the page rather than to each other.

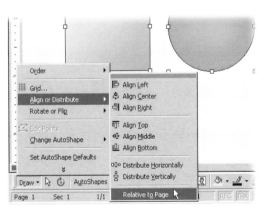

● Now on the **Drawing** toolbar, click **Draw** and then point to **Align or Distribute**. In the submenu select the page-alignment option that you want. In this example, **Align Top** is selected.

● The objects now have their tops aligned with the top of the page.

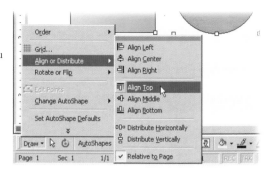

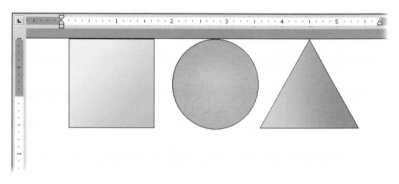

## THE ALIGN OR DISTRIBUTE OPTIONS

The options available in **Align or Distribute** produce these alignments with the **Relative to Page** option checked:

**Vertical alignments:**

**Align Left:** Objects aligned down the left-hand side of the page.

**Align Center:** Objects aligned down the center of the page.

**Align Right:** Objects aligned down the right-hand side of the page.

**Horizontal alignments:**

**Align Top:** Objects aligned across the top of the page.

**Align Middle:** Objects aligned across the middle of the page.

**Align Bottom:** Objects aligned across the foot of the page.

**Alignments by distribution** (for three or more objects):

**Distribute Horizontally:** Objects are aligned across the page with equal horizontal distances between them.

**Distribute Vertically:** Objects aligned down the page with equal vertical distances between them.

# ROTATING AND FLIPPING

An object can be rotated and/or flipped so that it adopts the orientation you want on the page. Rotation can be carried out either freehand by using the **Free Rotate** tool or precisely through 90 degrees using menu commands. The **Flip** command lets you completely reverse the orientation of an object either vertically or horizontally.

## 1 ROTATING TO ANY ANGLE

● Select the drawing object to be rotated and, on the **Drawing** toolbar, click on the **Free Rotate** tool.

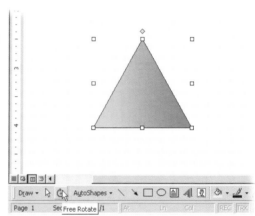

● The object now has four rotation handles around it. As you move the cursor onto the page, the object is accompanied by the rotation arrow.

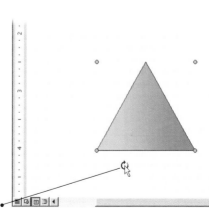

*Rotation arrow* ●

● Place the cursor over one of the handles of the object, hold down the left mouse button, and move the cursor in the required direction of rotation. A dotted outline appears as you rotate the object.

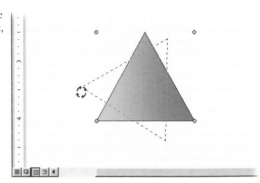

● When the amount of rotation has been reached, release the mouse button, and the object assumes its new orientation.
● You can either click on another object to rotate it, or press the [Esc] key to cancel the rotation arrow.

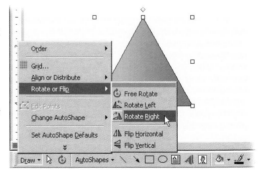

## 2 ROTATING BY 90 DEGREES

● Select the drawing object that you want to rotate, click on **Draw** on the **Drawing** toolbar and select **Rotate or Flip**.
● From the pop-up menu that appears, click on either the **Rotate Left** or the **Rotate Right** options.

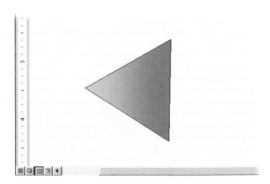

● The object is now turned through 90 degrees.

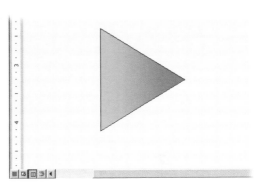

## 3 HORIZONTAL OR VERTICAL FLIP

● Select the object you want to flip, click on **Draw** on the **Drawing** toolbar, and select **Rotate or Flip**. Click on either **Flip Horizontal** or **Flip Vertical** on the submenu. The object is now turned through either its horizontal or vertical axis.

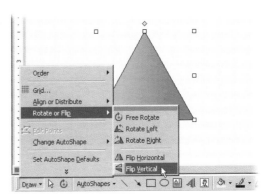

### *Rotate around a handle*

You can rotate an object or set of objects around the handle opposite the one you have selected by holding down the [Ctrl] key as you move the **Free Rotate** tool.

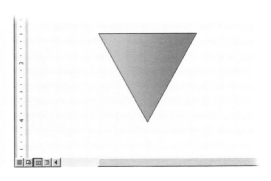

# DRAWINGS AND TEXT

There are many ways to combine drawing objects with text in Word. Text can be made to wrap around drawing objects and can be placed within drawing objects by using text boxes.

## TEXT BOXES

Using Word's text boxes could fill a chapter in its own right, but in relation to drawing objects, text boxes can be used to insert text into a drawing object precisely where you want it to be and can be formatted using all Word's features.

### 1 INSERTING A BANNER

● In this example, we'll use a banner from the **Auto Shapes** menu. Click on the **AutoShapes** button in the **Drawing** toolbar, move the cursor to **Stars and Banners**, and select a banner style from the pop-up menu.

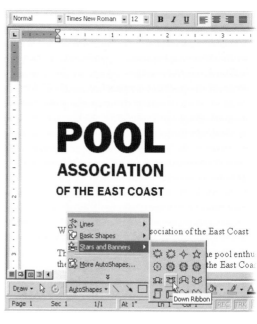

**⊘ AutoShapes menu**

● Position the cross hair in the document window where a corner of the banner is to appear, hold down the left mouse button and drag the mouse to draw the banner. Release the button when the banner is the size you want.

## 2 INSERTING A TEXT BOX
● Click on the Text Box button ▯ on the **Drawing** toolbar.

drag to insert a text box.  Text Box

*Text Box button* ●

**㉕ Text box**

● Move the cursor, which is now a cross hair, onto the banner, hold down the left mouse button and drag until the box is the required size. Release the mouse button and the text box appears with a blinking cursor ready for text to be typed in.

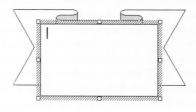

● Now simply type in your text.

## 3 FORMATTING THE TEXT

● The text appears in the default font, usually Times New Roman, and is left-aligned, which isn't appropriate for banner text.
● To format the text, begin by highlighting it.

● Select a font from the
**Font** drop-down menu
in the **Formatting** toolbar.
Here, **Gill Sans MT** is being
selected.

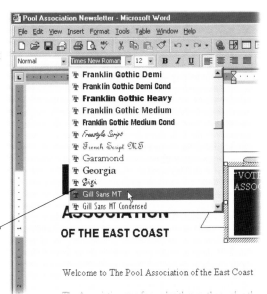

*Font being selected*

● The text now appears in
the selected font, one that is
more suitable for stand-
alone text at the head of a
document.

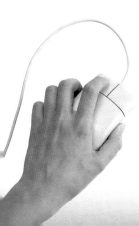

**❷ Font
selector**

● The next step is to center the text. With the text still selected, click on the **Center** button on the **Formatting** toolbar.

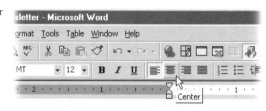

● The text is now centered, but the font size, usually the default size of 12pt, is too small for a banner.

● The text should still be highlighted, so click on the down arrow to the right of the font size box ◌ and select a larger size. In this case **16pt** is selected.

*Font size selection* ●

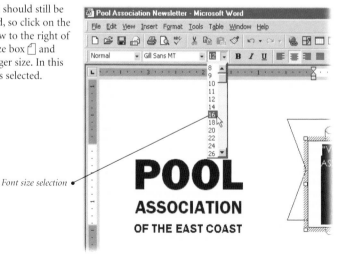

8

❸ **Font size selector**

● The text in the box now repositions itself to accommodate the larger font size.

ciation of the East Coast

:d with you, the pool enthusiast, in mind. We began with
up and down the East Coast to get to know and play one

● Once the formatting of the text is complete, click off the text box to view the results of the work so far.

ciation of the East Coast

:d with you, the pool enthusiast, in mind. We began with
up and down the East Coast to get to know and play one

## 4 HIDING THE BORDER

● By default, text boxes have a black border. If you want to remove it, highlight the text box, click on **Format** in the Menu bar and select **Text Box**.

● Click on the **Colors and Lines** tab if it is not already displayed. Click on the arrow to the right of **Color** and select **No Line** from the drop-down menu.

### *Another way to hide the border*

Make the text box border color the same as the fill color of the drawing object by clicking on the **Line Color** button. If the object has no fill color, make the border white.

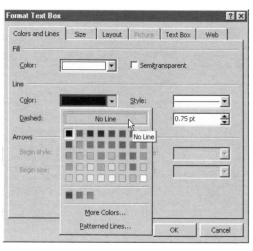

● Click on **OK**, and the text box no longer has a border.

## 5 CONCEALING THE TEXT BOX

● If the banner is given a fill color ⌐, as we have here, the box stands out from the banner because the text box has its own color. This color can be removed to conceal the presence of the text box completely. Select the text box by clicking on it.

● Click on the arrow to the right of the **Fill Color** button ⌐ on the **Drawing** toolbar and select **No Fill**.

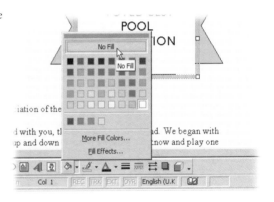

● The text box now becomes transparent and its presence is no longer apparent.

Using
26 Colors

**28** Fill
9 color

## CLICK AND TYPE

You can type directly into a drawing object without inserting a text box by right-clicking inside the object and selecting **Add Text** from the pop-up menu. Each drawing object has a preselected location within it where text will appear. Also, it is possible to change the margins of the text. Using a text box superimposed on a drawing object gives you greater control over the precise positioning of your text because the box itself can be moved easily.

## 6 CHANGING THE MARGINS

● You can increase or decrease the distance between the borders of a text box and the text it contains. Select the text box by clicking in it and select **Text Box** from the **Format** menu.

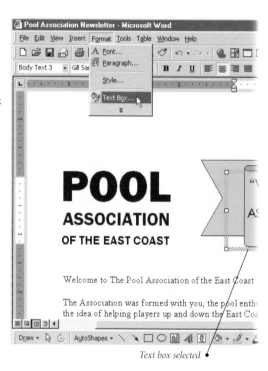

*Text box selected ●*

● The **Format Text Box** dialog box opens. Click on the **Text Box** tab and alter the four margin options as required.

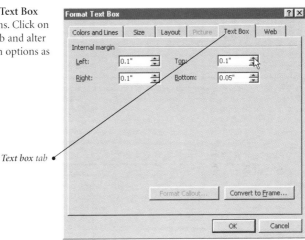

*Text box tab* ●

● Click on **OK** and the text now occupies the new position in the box that you

specified in the margin settings.

● The **Format Text Box**

dialog box also allows you to change other features such as line style.

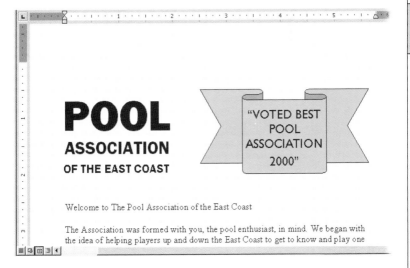

# MAKING LOGO GRAPHICS

A number of techniques have now been dealt with in the book, and it is now possible to combine them into a simple, but effective, logo. The examples shown here are intended to be purely illustrative and show the results rather than the steps.

## 1 INSERTING THE SHAPES
● The first step here is to insert a circle and a triangle into the current document. A circle can be created by selecting the **Oval** tool  and holding down the ⌨Shift key while drawing the object.

## 2 ADDING FILL COLORS
● The fills used here are two-color fills using white and the second color. The shading style chosen is **From center** .

## 3 INSERTING A THIRD ELEMENT
● A third element, a smaller circle, is inserted close to the existing objects for later use.

## 4 INSERTING A TEXT BOX

● A text box is added to the document containing the figure 8, which has been formatted in **18pt Helvetica**, and centered. Its fill color has been removed so that it is transparent ⌐.

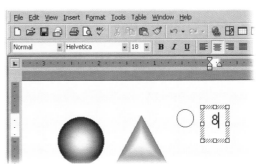

## 5 COMBINING THE ELEMENTS

● The separate elements are now being brought together. The small circle has been place over the black ball, and the text box is now being dragged across. The figure 8 will rejoin the box once it has been dropped into place.

## 6 THE COMPLETED LOGO

● With the separate elements combined, the logo is now finished.

Welcome to The Pool Association of the East Coast

# TEXT WRAPPING

Any one of the drawing objects that can be created by using Word can be placed anywhere within a passage of text. The text itself can wrap around the drawing object in one of several ways, which are available via a menu. In addition, the margins between the text and the drawing object can be set very precisely.

## 1 WRAP TEXT AROUND OBJECT

● First place the drawing object over the text that is to wrap around it.

● Select the drawing object by clicking on it so that its handles are being shown.

● Select the **AutoShape** option from the **Format** menu. This option contains the majority of formatting commands you will need for drawing objects.

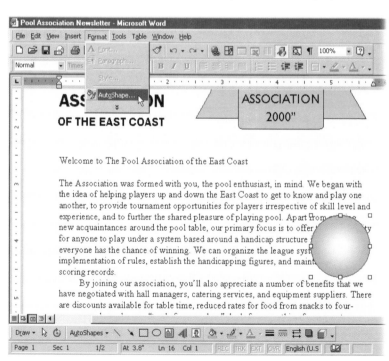

● The **Format AutoShape** dialog box opens. Click on the **Layout** tab.

*Layout tab* ●

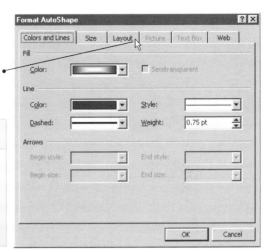

**NUDGING AN OBJECT**

A drawing object can be moved in small steps by selecting it and pressing the ← → ↑ ↓ keys on the keyboard to fine-tune its location.

● There are five possible options for relating the object to the text. In this case, we'll select the **Tight** option to illustrate how the text can flow around the object.

● With the **Tight** option selected, click on **OK**.

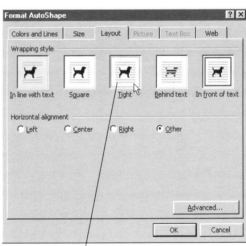

*The **Tight** option* ●

● The text flows around the drawing object by following its shape.

the East Coast

u, the pool enthusiast, in mind. We began with
wn the East Coast to get to know and play one
tunities for players irrespective of skill level and
pleasure of playing pool. Apart
ind the pool table, our primary
nyone to play under a system
which everyone has the
the league system, oversee
n the handicapping figures, and

*The text follows the* ●
*shape of the object*

'll also appreciate a number of benefits that we
catering services, and equipment suppliers. There

## 2 CONTROLLING THE MARGINS

● It is also possible to use more advanced controls, such as adjusting the margins between an object and its surrounding text.

● Select the drawing object, select **AutoShape** from the **Format** menu, click the **Layout** tab in the **Format AutoShape** dialog box, click on the **Advanced** button, and click on the **Text Wrapping** tab.

*Text wrapping tab* ●

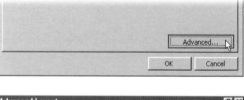

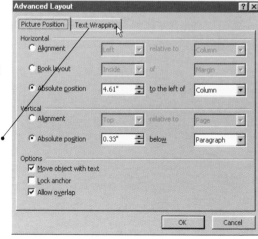

● Click on **Top and bottom** in the **Wrapping style** options.

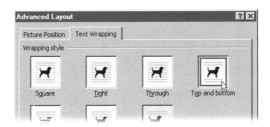

● Set the **Top** and **Bottom** margin settings by clicking on the spin buttons in the **Distance from text** section at bottom-left and click on OK.

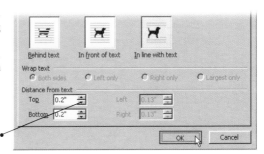

*Margin settings spin buttons* ●

● The object is now separated from the text by the selected distances.

### USING TABLES

You can insert graphics into table cells and insert text into adjacent cells to align with the graphic – either horizontally or vertically. You can increase or decrease the distance between text and graphics by changing the size of the table cells and the alignment of the text in the cells.

**ASSOCIATION 2000"**

Association of the East Coast

ormed with you, the pool enthusiast, in mind. We began with yers up and down the East Coast to get to know and play one

rnament opportunities for players irrespective of skill level and her the shared pleasure of playing pool. Apart from making

## 3 LAYERING TEXT AND DRAWINGS

● There may be occasions when you want to "layer" the text and the graphic associated with it. Begin by selecting the drawing object and select **AutoShape** from the **Formatting** menu to open the **Format AutoShape** dialog box.

● In the **Format Auto-Shape** dialog box, click on the **Layout** tab and click on the **Behind text** rectangle.

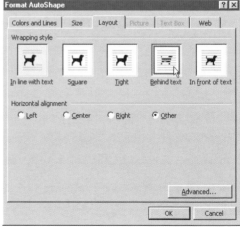

● Click on **OK**, and the text flows over the drawing object. Once having seen the effect, it's apparent that the colors used with the text need to be chosen carefully. Dark colors cannot be used as they will make the text unreadable.

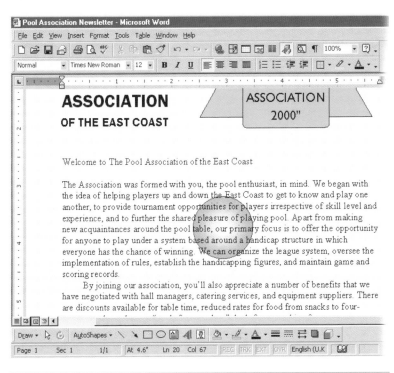

## CAN'T SELECT IMAGE?

If the object that has been placed behind the text is completely covered by the text, you will not be able to select it again simply by clicking on it. To select the object, first click on another drawing object to select it (or create a temporary object if there are no others in your document and select it). Hold down the ⬆ Shift key and press the Tab⇆ key repeatedly to cycle through the objects until the object behind the text becomes highlighted. Then select **In front of text** in the **Layers** tab of the **Format AutoShape** dialog box. Once the object is in front, you can change the object as required.

# ANCHORING TEXT AND DRAWING OBJECTS

Inserting a drawing object into text links it to the paragraph immediately preceding it. This link is indicated by an anchor icon in the left-hand margin, which you can see when you turn on the formatting marks. The anchor icon is at the start of the paragraph, and it is this paragraph to which you can permanently attach the object.

### SELECTING THE OBJECT

● You may want a drawing object to move when the paragraph to which it is linked is moved. The paragraph may move position, for example, when text is inserted nearer the beginning of the document. First click on the object to select it.

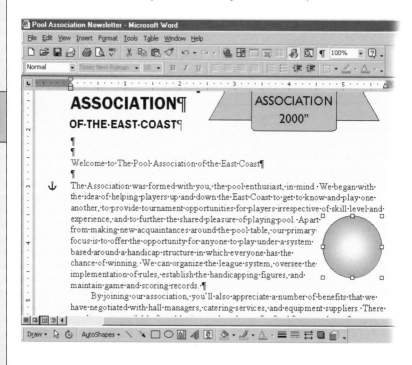

● Select **AutoShape** from the **Format** menu , click on the **Layout** tab at the top of the **Format Auto-Shape** dialog box, and click on the **Advanced** button to display the **Advanced Layout** dialog box.

● Click on the **Picture Position** tab at the top of the dialog box.

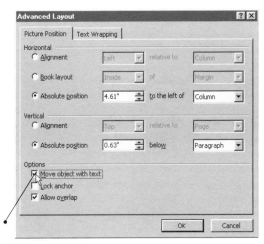

## MOVE OBJECT WITH TEXT

● In the **Options** section, click in the **Move object with text** check box to insert a checkmark.

*Move object with text* •
*check box*

● Click on **OK** twice to close the dialog boxes. If the anchor icon is not visible, then click on **Show/hide** in the **Standard** toolbar.

64 **Layering text and drawings**

● The drawing object is now anchored to that paragraph.

● You can still move the object to any new location within the paragraph and

the text will continue to move to accommodate the object and flow around it.

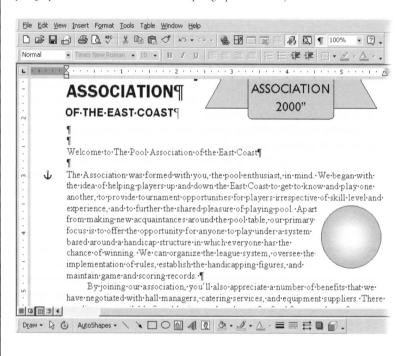

## KEEPING TEXT AND OBJECTS ANCHORED

When you move a drawing object to another paragraph, the anchor icon disappears from that paragraph and reappears at the beginning of the paragraph that now contains the drawing object. In many cases, this may not present any difficulty, but there may be times when you want to move the object while making sure that it remains anchored to its original paragraph and will move with it. This is simply done by checking the **Lock** **anchor** check box in the **Options** section of the **Advanced** settings of the **Format AutoShape Layout** tab. Now, no matter how far you move the object within the document, it still moves with that paragraph.

● Now as the text is added to the first paragraph, the second paragraph moves down the page as usual, but now the drawing object attached to the paragraph also moves with it and retains its precise position within the paragraph.

OF THE EAST COAST

¶
¶
Welcome·to·The·Pool·Association·of·the·East·Coast.·We·greatly·appreciate·your·
enquiry·and·hope·that·the·enclosed¶

¶
The·Association·was·formed·with·you,·the·pool·enthusiast,·in·mind.·We·began·with·
the·idea·of·helping·players·up·and·down·the·East·Coast·to·get·to·know·and·play·one·
another,·to·provide·tournament·opportunities·for·players·irrespective·of·skill·level·and·
experience,·and·to·further·the·shared·pleasure·of·playing·pool.·Apart·
from·making·new·acquaintances·around·the·pool·table,·our·primary·
focus·is·to·offer·the·opportunity·for·anyone·to·play·under·a·system·
based·around·a·handicap·structure·in·which·everyone·has·the·
chance·of·winning.·We·can·organize·the·league·system,·oversee·the·
implementation·of·rules,·establish·the·handicapping·figures,·and·
maintain·game·and·scoring·records.·¶
        By·joining·our·association,·you'll·also·appreciate·a·number·of·benefits·that·we·
have·negotiated·with·hall·managers,·catering·services,·and·equipment·suppliers.·There·

● The completed additional text has been accommodated at the start of the document and all the following text and graphics have moved down.

**OF·THE·EAST·COAST**¶                    2000''¶

¶
¶
Welcome·to·The·Pool·Association·of·the·East·Coast.·We·greatly·appreciate·your·
enquiry·and·hope·that·the·enclosed·information·is·of·use·to·you.·If·you·have·any·
queries·whatsoever,·please·do·not·hesitate·to·contact·us.·We·would·like·to·take·the·
opportunity·of·pointing·out·that·our·membership·is·approaching·the·one-thousand·
mark,·and·that·the·first·five·members·to·join·once·we·have·passed·that·figure·will·be·
entitled·to·life-time·membership.¶

¶
The·Association·was·formed·with·you,·the·pool·enthusiast,·in·mind.·We·began·with·
the·idea·of·helping·players·up·and·down·the·East·Coast·to·get·to·know·and·play·one·
another,·to·provide·tournament·opportunities·for·players·irrespective·of·skill·level·and·
experience,·and·to·further·the·shared·pleasure·of·playing·pool.·Apart·
from·making·new·acquaintances·around·the·pool·table,·our·primary·
focus·is·to·offer·the·opportunity·for·anyone·to·play·under·a·system·
based·around·a·handicap·structure·in·which·everyone·has·the·
chance·of·winning.·We·can·organize·the·league·system,·oversee·the·

# GLOSSARY

**ALIGNMENT**
In the context of drawing objects, this refers to the edges of objects that are aligned vertically or horizontally either with one another or with the edges of the page.

**ANCHOR ICON**
The position of the anchor icon indicates the paragraph on the page to which drawing object is linked.

**AUTOSHAPES**
A collection of predesigned shapes and drawing tools used to create drawing objects in a document.

**CROSS HAIR CURSOR**
When a drawing tool has been selected and the cursor is moved onto the document, it changes to a cross hair to indicate where a line or shape will be positioned.

**DIALOG BOX**
A rectangle that appears on the screen and prompts you for a reply, usually with buttons, for example, **OK** or **Cancel**.

**DOCKED TOOLBAR**
A toolbar that is locked in position at one of the edges of the document window.

**DRAWING OBJECT**
Any graphic or drawn shape that has been placed on a page.

**DRAWING TOOLBAR**
The toolbar that contains the tools to create drawing objects and the controls to alter their appearance by adding effects and changing their order.

**EDIT POINTS**
Points at which a curve or a freeform changes direction on the page. More commonly referred to as vertexes.

**FILL**
Coloring a drawing object by selecting a "fill" color.

**FLIPPING**
Changing the orientation of a drawing object by rotating it around either its vertical or horizontal axis.

**FLOATING TOOLBAR**
When a toolbar is selected for display, it may appear in the document window unattached to any of the edges of the window, this is known as "floating" and is the opposite of "docked."

**FOLDER**
A folder stores files and other folders to keep files organized.

**FREEFORM**
A drawing tool that is used to create both straight and curved lines.

**FONT**
The typeface in which text appears onscreen and when it is printed out.

**GRADIENT**
A gradient describes the shading of one color into another color in a drawing object.

**LINE STYLE**
Alternative thicknesses or "weight" of lines around a drawing object.

**MARGIN**
The space between the text and the edge of the paper, or a drawing object that has been embedded in the text. There are four margins: top, bottom, left, and right.

**PRINT LAYOUT VIEW**
One of four possible ways of viewing a document in Word. This view displays the document and its contents in exactly the same way as it will appear when printed.

**RESIZING**
Dragging one of the handles surrounding a drawing object to change its shape.

**RULER**
Indicators at the top and left of the screen, with marks in inches or centimeters. Rulers also show the indents, tabs, and margins of the text.

**SHADING**
Also known as a "gradient," this effect shows one color gradually changing to another.

**TEXT WRAPPING**
The flow of text around an object embedded in the text. There are several different options from which to choose the way in which the text flows around an object.

**VERTEX**
A point at which a curved line or a freeform changes direction. Vertexes can be added and deleted, and can be used to alter the degree to which a line curves.

# INDEX

# ACKNOWLEDGMENTS

PUBLISHER'S ACKNOWLEDGMENTS
Dorling Kindersley would like to thank the following:
Paul Mattock of APM, Brighton, for commissioned photography.
Microsoft Corporation for permission to reproduce screens
from within Microsoft® Word 2000.

*Every effort has been made to trace the copyright holders.*
*The publisher apologizes for any unintentional omissions and would be pleased,*
*in such cases, to place an acknowledgment in future editions of this book.*

Microsoft® is a registered trademark of Microsoft Corporation
in the United States and/or other countries.